The Office Book™
DESIGN SERIES

D0906570

Office Furniture

Susan S. Szenasy
Consulting Editor: Edith Siroto

Facts On File

Facts On File, Inc.
460 Park Avenue South
New York, New York 10016

FOREST PARK LIBRARY

A QUARTO BOOK

First published in 1984 by Facts On File, Inc.
460 Park Avenue South, New York, N.Y. 10016

Copyright © 1984 by
Quarto Marketing Ltd.

All rights reserved under the
Pan-American and International Copyright Conventions.
No part of this book may be reproduced
or utilized in any form or by any means, electronic or
mechanical, including photocopying, recording or by any
information storage and retrieval system, without permission
in writing from Quarto Marketing Ltd.

Library of Congress Cataloging in Publication Data
Szenasy, Susan S.
Office furniture.
Bibliography: p. 94
Includes index.
1. Office furniture. 2. Office decoration. I. Title.
HF5521.S94 1984 749 83-5652

ISBN 0-87196-811-8
ISBN 0-87196-810-X (pbk.)

OFFICE FURNITURE
was produced and prepared by
Quarto Marketing Ltd.
212 Fifth Avenue
New York, NY 10010

Art Director: Richard Boddy
Managing Editor: Naomi Black
Editorial Assistant: Mary Forsell

Typeset by BPE Graphics, Inc.
Color separations by Hong Kong Scanner Craft Company Ltd.
Printed and bound in Hong Kong by Leefung-Asco Printers Ltd.

TO RJM FOR BEING THERE

MY THANKS to all the kind people in the
furniture showrooms for allowing me to roam freely
through miles of desks, chairs, and sofas; for
demonstrating the workings of "ergonomic" designs;
and for providing me with lots of food for thought.

MY SPECIAL THANKS to furniture manufacturers
and their public relations specialists, to craftsmen
and their gallery representatives, for supplying the
photographs assembled in this book.

CONTENTS

Systems and Craftsmen

The one important point to be made about office furniture in the 1980s is its potential for fitting the needs of each individual. Whether using mass-produced component parts that assemble into furniture or handcrafted pieces made to order, it is possible today to furnish an office that suits each person's work as well as their style and status requirements.

Desks made to order from slabs and wedges that hover over wired beams that channel the office's electrical lifeline; chairs that can be adjusted to a person's height, size, and working habits; filing cabinets that are tailored to the specialized storage needs of each office—all are available in many choices. In all, the principal of ergonomics (from the Greek *ergo*, meaning "work," and *nomos*, meaning "laws"), also called human engineering, is at work. These terms express the growing tendency to include scientific data in the design process. The concern with our body movements and our emotional responses to the world around us is expressed in much of the publicity that accompanies each new product introduction. The proof of the promises is in each of our experiences with the furniture.

The chair, because it comes in direct and intimate contact with the human body, has proven to be the most difficult design assignment. The thousands of chairs that are being made prove the designer's dilemma in producing a product for an amorphous market where the choices are made by an individual with unique needs for support, movement, size, and aesthetic expression.

The very personal nature of the chair begins to explain the lingering appeal of well-known designs even as many new ones are introduced each year. The steady stream of revivals announces a new interest in the work of designers who explored the organic, the decorative, and the stylish at a time

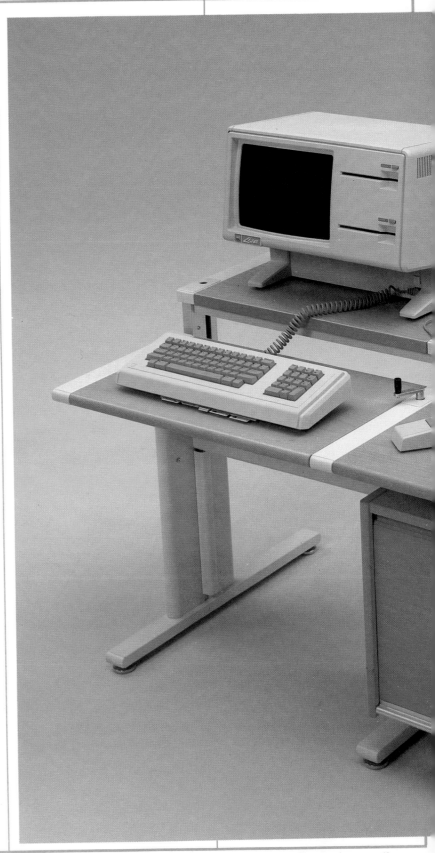

Photograph courtesy Krueger

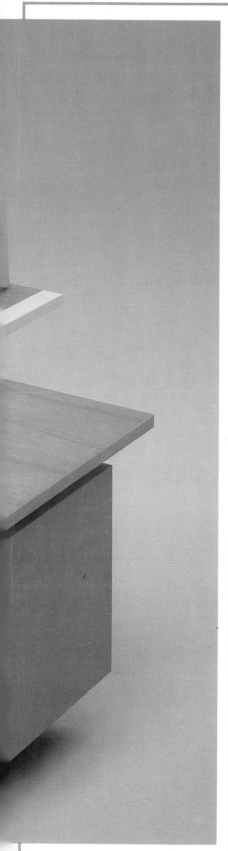

Graves armchair

DESIGNER: Michael Graves

MANUFACTURER: Sunar, Waterloo, Ontario

The award winner that combines rich materials like bird's-eye maple, lacquer, and silk or leather challenges the craftsman's abilities to build exquisitely detailed, emotionally satisfying forms. It waits to be put into production.

Databord 920

MANUFACTURER: Krueger, Green Bay, Wisconsin

Furniture made from a system of beams, posts, boards, and containers builds into a desk that accommodates the current tools of office work. Top height can be adjusted by a hand crank; the suspended file drawer has a decorative tambour door.

when these were outlawed by the highly vocal purists. The designs of the early twentieth century bring a new richness of form, material, and above all, inspiration, to the marketplace. In addition, many of these reproductions require the revival of skills that mass production nearly eliminated.

The search for personally meaningful skills has given birth to a new generation of young men and women who make their living by the design and crafting of furniture. Whether driven by the need for artistic expression that goes beyond the emotions and explores questions of function or by the joy of doing work that requires a highly refined understanding of materials and forms, the new craftsmen are producing exquisite work that many galleries sell as art and museums add to their collections.

Taking inspiration from the past three thousand years—often intrigued by the work of the moderns, which is either in production or in the pages of many beautiful books and magazines that are currently available—the designers of the 1980s see a world rich with options. Their work can enrich and enliven our own options.

Photograph by Bill Kontzias

Adjustable Desks and Storage

The desk used to be a surface for writing and a box for storing documents. Now the desk has become a surface that supports machines that can store documents in some mysterious space that most of us can't fathom. It has become a scaffold, a construction of post and beam and slab and container. Its designers talk about "wire management" as they envision an enormous electronic coil running through a vast hive of "data processing stations."

The talk about the people who operate the machines and use the desk is as abstract as the work they're required to perform. They are "operators," "word processors," and "users" who are under the constant scrutiny of "human factors researchers" whose findings, in turn, help create "environments" that produce "worker efficiencies," which, until now, have not been measured to anyone's satisfaction. This, then, is the case of the missing person. The poet in us, the dreamer, the very essence of us, seems to have been left out of the tabulations.

But there is a somewhat hopeful side to this dismal accounting. The hope lies in the maze of component parts, modules, and standardized elements to which furniture has been reduced. Like the brick that holds in its simple form the promise of a home, so the new furniture's building blocks can be assembled to fit a person's needs. In order to make that happen, everyone concerned needs to participate. The process is a fragile one. It may come apart at any of its many joints. It requires no less of every person—from the one who designs the product to the one who uses it—than to understand his or her place in a rapidly changing world.

Instead of devising products for a pale, statistical ghost who makes X number of moves in space Y to complete task Z, some designers are envisioning their work being used by the people they know. An image of mother at the CRT or dad in the boardroom or a buddy in the lunchroom can invest a designer's work with personal meaning. Such involved thinking has been known to produce things that are clearly understood by many people, who, after all, are somebody's mother, father, as well as friend, in addition to being blips on a chart.

The very presence of products that have that mysteriously personal appeal to large numbers of people is an encouragement. It signifies the existence of industrial designers who like people; manufacturers who can see their customers as more than mere consumers at the end of the assembly line; sales people who can demonstrate the possibilities designed into the product; interior designers who take interest in their real clients—the people who will use the office; and the workers themselves, who can talk with honesty and clarity about what they aspire to and need for the accomplishment of their jobs.

Such ideal worlds, by their own definition, understate the realities of office life with its complex power struggles and fossilized organization charts. But they also confirm the fact that a whole new range of products can exist and may even help ease some of those tensions, if used with intelligence and imagination.

The new desk—or "systems furniture," as it is often called—accepts human variety as a fact of life. Unlike the old steel desk, with its fixed-in-place files, that required the worker to adapt to it; the new desk can be made-to-order for the person who uses it. It can be adapted to people as different in their work habits as those who scatter papers around them, or those who line things up neatly, or those who confer regularly, or those who use office machines extensively.

Most systems are built on hollow metal beams and posts that channel the wiring from computers, desk lamps, telephones, typewriters, pencil sharpeners, or any other gadgets that are about to show up in the office. This structural system—often called by such organic-sounding names as spine or arterial passageway—receives tabletops of various sizes and shapes, some of which can be adjusted in height; file cabinets of varied capacities; niches and nodes of many functions.

The new desk, with its ability to extend the work area, has contributed to the rethinking of office storage solutions, as have the proliferation of a new generation of accessories that

Photograph by Rudolph Janu

accompany electronic equipment, such as EDP printouts, magnetic tapes, floppy disks, and platters.

The result is a filing cabinet that has become a "storage system." It can build whole walls of storage or stand as a room divider, with access from both sides. It can roll around the floor or hang from underneath the desk or from a divider panel. The variety of exterior shapes and colors is matched by the flexibility of its interior dividers, racks, hooks, rods, sleeves, and drawers.

While they were being reworked to accommodate the changing technology of the office, the desk and the filing cabinet have also been "humanized." This chilling little word is often used to describe the warming and softening of colors, the rounding of edges, and texturings like tambour doors, all of which make the new furniture easy to look at and pleasant to the human touch.

Race system

DESIGNER: Douglas Ball

MANUFACTURER: Sunar, Waterloo, Ontario

"Wire management" is not a small problem for a teen who tunes into the universe. His electronic office/bedroom is organized on a system of posts and beams that channel all wires to the wall outlet. Shelves, table-tops, and cabinets are hung from upholstered panels. An added feature of mobility is achieved by the rolling chair and storage cabinets. Interior design by Madeline Rossof of Contract Interiors for Business, Chicago.

The Burdick Group

DESIGNER: Bruce Burdick

MANUFACTURER: Herman Miller, Zeeland, Michigan

When it was introduced in 1981, this system of components announced a new approach to desk and storage design.

The various parts build up around a hollow-core, extruded aluminum beam that accepts the electrical wiring of office machinery. Like a bird's delicate wings, slim but strong support brackets attach to the central vertebrae of the beam. These supports cantilever upward, for holding work surfaces above the beam, or downward, for organizing storage containers below the beam.

The work surfaces come in rectangles of several sizes, circles, and half circles. They are made of materials that can satisfy tastes from the humble to the somewhat pretentious, but never ostentatious: black laminate, clear glass, oak, and marble. Surfaces that are meant to hold keyboards and typewriters are hung lower than the rest. Those that support large office machines can extend and pivot.

The containers, uniformly made of a soft-feeling black polyurethane material, include filing drawers, paper trays, trays for large and small phones, catalog and book organizers, easellike props for reading matter, movable plant or memorabilia stands, and waste bins.

Showing its high technology origins in every detail, the furniture nevertheless conveys a friendly, if not warm, feeling of individuality. This begins at the sinewy, three-toed birdlike foot on which it stands.

Although the manufacturer's marketing effort has been directed toward the executive and the professional, the Burdick Group adapts comfortably to other workers' needs as well. Here is how a receptionist/secretary might combine a 7-foot and a 5-foot 6-inch beam into an L-shaped desk.

The core of the system, a polished aluminum beam, can be joined at any point by another beam. The polyurethane end-cap protects passersby and completes the machined smoothness of the system.

Supporting brackets for the work surfaces snap on the beam at any point, just as the small plant stand can move along the beam.

Like the legs of a lunar landing module, the brackets suspended from the beam secure the storage cabinets that hover above the floor.

The machine table expands to conform to the size of the electronic equipment it supports. It also pivots.

Photographs courtesy Herman Miller

At the reception area, wood veneer tops are assembled as a traditional L-shaped typist's desk.

Kinetics Desk

DESIGNERS: Paolo Favaretto and Jim Hayward

MANUFACTURER: Kinetics Furniture, Rexdale, Ontario

The hovering trestle table with its slim top is combined with a wire-carrying beam and movable file drawers to create custom-built desks for electronic offices. The beam is designed to contain two segregated channels: one for electrical circuits, the other for communications cables. It can be linked together to support desks in a row (as many as ten, with wires and cables feeding in from one point) or in the round, or many combinations in between.

The desk tops have extruded aluminum channels on their undersides, which fit into brackets that snap into the beam, which is supported by tubular steel legs. These trestle legs or T-braces can be leveled by turning the small, knurled wheel built into their slim, rounded feet. The steel support as well as the metal files, which are made wide enough to accept EDP printouts, can be finished in twenty different colors.

In addition to the many options for individual expressions that the colors offer, there are several choices of material for tabletops, including tinted glass, wood veneer, and laminates. A special detail affirms the furniture's "industrial style": the feet, bellows, and hub of the support structure are a smooth, molded plastic.

The "modesty panel," in matching veneers or contrasting colors, can be hinged to the desk top, which protects itself and its user by the resilient edging that's molded into a hard plastic core. The hubcap conceals the mechanical interior of the wired beam.

For the executive, two tinted-glass tops can be arranged as work table and storage credenza. The support structure can match or coordinate with the color of the movable metal files.

Photographs courtesy Kinetics

COM System

DESIGNERS: F. Frascaroli and C. Biondi

MANUFACTURER: Krueger Contract Division, Green Bay, Wisconsin

A single desk can be made into a work-top, machine support, and a conference table. The desk lamp attaches to the electrical outlet of the beam that supports the top.

A new twist is given to the basic idea of a beam that supports and suspends various modules that build up to fit the work and storage requirements of office workers. The options include several different legs; beam connectors that are radiused, Y-shaped, or cruciform; file drawers on wheels or console-type with top openings; larger storage units including lateral files and wardrobes; and accessories like the desk lamp with its digital clock.

In addition to building desks that may undulate into infinity or arrange into more complex shapes, the components can also be used to put together tra-ditional desks with panel legs and fronts. All desks, however, are designed around the wire-carrying steel beam, that channels power through the legs to the floor outlets.

The furniture strives hard to live up to its name: COM is trade language for "customer's own material." Tops with their shapes of straight or round-edged rectangles, quarter circles, semicircles, circles, and several wedges are made of black or sand-colored laminate, oak veneer, smoked glass, high gloss lacquer, and lacquer with leather inset. The system is meant to have an appeal at every level of the organization.

To comfortably coordinate hand and eye movement for the operator, the console is placed at standard table height while the keyboard is recessed and cantilevered from the power beam.

The flexible bellows mechanism allows the angle of light from the desk lamp to be adjusted. The lamp's stem contains a digital clock.

One large, continuing desk, which is tailored to the work needs of each individual, may be built for a group who needs to share information.

Photographs courtesy Krueger

Activity Center Module

DESIGNER: Karl Dittert

MANUFACTURER: Probber + VOKO, Fall River, Massachusetts

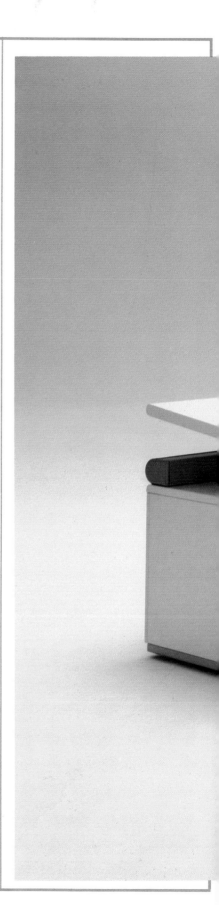

The issue of body movement is thought about in this modular system that builds furniture on a steel, wire-carrying beam and post support. The design is reminiscent of adjustable drafting tables. While corner wedges, machine supports, and other work tops remain stationary, others tilt and raise to the desired height, up to 44½ inches.

There is a no-nonsense quality about the furniture when the soft-gray laminate tops are used. This deliberate coolness is warmed up when the oak, walnut, or mahogany veneers are chosen.

An extensive storage and room divider panel system has been designed to go with what can become a wrap-around work area with horizontal and vertical dimensions tailored to the individual. In addition to the small cabinets that take care of immediate filing needs—usually placed under desk tops—or a slightly larger unit whose top-access tambour door adds to the work surface area, there is "Superdrawer." It looks like any

Desk height can be raised to conform to a person's seated or standing position by pressing the button on the right foot of the desk. A knob under the work surface can be turned to adjust its tilt.

high file cabinet, but its expanded storage area can hold the files of two workers, on either side of it, and is accessible to both without disturbing the privacy of either. Low and high tambour door storage cabinets can act as additional work surfaces and space dividers. Bookshelves, swing door cabinets, and movable walls that have electrical outlets, come in various sizes.

A metal rack clamps onto the desk to suspend paper and book organizers, telephones, lamps, and pencil drawers above the work surface.

The blue metal channel, which supports modular work surfaces, provides ample room for the wires of office machinery and lamps. The weighted metal legs carry the wires to floor outlets. A file unit with a tambour door top, extends the work surface.

Drawings and photograph courtesy Harvey Probber

Cameron

DESIGNER: Douglas Ball

MANUFACTURER: Sunar,
Waterloo, Ontario

As office machines proliferate, some designers react by "going back to basics," perhaps on a hunch that familiar furniture can make the transition into the electronic age easier.

The man who designed Race, the open plan system (see page 9), which has influenced the "wire management" of the current crop of office furniture, is going back to using such comfortable words as "desks, tables, run-offs, and credenzas," to describe furniture that is clearly all of these things.

From two basic modules, 28 inches and 26 inches high, it is possible to compose desks and tables with storage on one side or both, as well as small and large credenzas. Connecting tops may help combine these units into an alphabet of shapes, from C to T.

The familiar storage cabinet can now accept hanging files for large-size printout sheets and other bulky computer products. As some retreats will do, this one has produced an advance: The ⅜-inch slots between the end panel and the top allow up to four thin wires to be threaded under the desk's surface, down to the floor outlets. This unassuming little slot may become a new symbol for purists: The beautiful mahogany or maple tops do not have to be drilled with wire holes even if they function in a wired society.

Photographs courtesy Sunar

A run-off, which crosses over a long, shared desk surface, has a turntable that allows two people to share one computer.

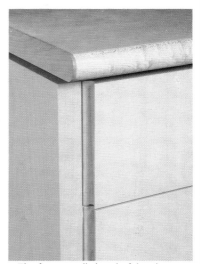

The finger-pull detail of the drawers and the slim, solid wood edging on the tops add a touch of elegance to durability.

The thin slot between the pedestal and the top accommodates wires, eliminating the need to drill through the wood top.

Uniwall

DESIGNER: Douglas Ball

MANUFACTURER: Sunar, Waterloo, Ontario

Uniwall file and storage cabinets line the walls and support the Teletype machines at the ABC Newsroom in Washington, D.C. The lateral files have slim channels on the sides of the drawers, replacing the frontal drawer-pull, which could add to the visual clutter of busy, open offices. Sunar's Race system desk tops and divider panels, suspended from a channel that supports electrical wiring, keeps this vibrant room from entangling in its communications lines. Interior design by Anne May Kearns.

Top photograph by Mark Segal

S-Drawers

DESIGNER: Douglas Ball

MANUFACTURER: Sunar, Waterloo, Ontario

The basic two-drawer desk pedestal file has been turned into a metal mobile unit, which can line up with its companions to form an executive credenza or to roll top-secret information around the office.

Bottom photographs courtesy Sunar

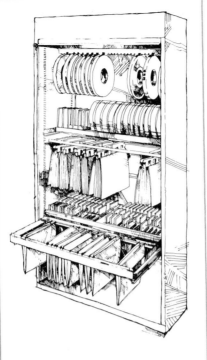

Emtech Storage Components

MANUFACTURER: GF Furniture Systems, Youngstown, Ohio

With the aid of thirty-five different components, the familiar metal storage cabinets (these come in three different heights) can be tailored to an office's electronic media storage needs. Behind its fashionable tambour door, the cabinet can organize information with the aid of hanging tape rails, magnetic tape racks, lateral file rails, pull-out shelves for cassette trays, and at least ten other standard elements.

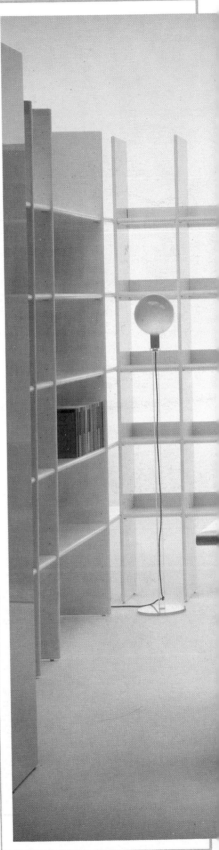

Space System

DESIGNER: Aldo van den Nieuwelaar

MANUFACTURER: Beylerian, New York, New York

A series of cabinet units in many widths, varying in height from 53 to 95 inches, have radiused or obliquely curved tops over which tambour doors slide when opened. Each cabinet can reveal different combinations of interior fittings, which may include file drawers, pull-out tops, vertical slots, small cubby holes, and mirrored backs. The shells of the units are made of medium-density fiberboard, enamel-painted in white, black, blue, two kinds of reds and grays. The shutters, in the same color choices, are vacuum formed of polystyrene. It is possible to combine a shell of one color with a shutter of another color and fittings of still another color.

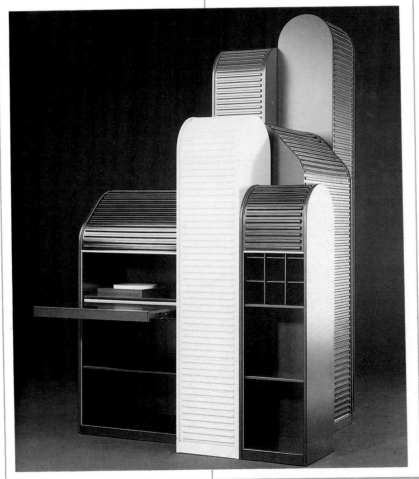

Top photograph and drawing courtesy GF Furniture Systems, Inc.

Bottom photograph courtesy Beylerian

Olinto

DESIGNER: Kazuhide Takahama

MANUFACTURER: B&B America,
New York, New York

*A shelving module about 11 inches
deep and 62 inches high can extend
its use with the aid of several cabinet
units (low, medium, medium-high,
and high). Open shelves may
alternate with open or closed
cabinets. Their hinged doors can be
made of glass or match the color of
the shelves (a glossy polyester white,
black, or red). A complete working
system may be built from shallow and
deep drawers, adjustable shelves,
closets with hang-rods and hooks, a
bar unit, and a writing shelf.*

Photograph courtesy B&B America

Mobile and Resilient Chairs

The imprint of the human form is increasingly visible on office chairs. Trim, contoured, smooth-skinned, and mobile, these chairs have become natural expressions of the sedentary body at work in a health-conscious society. As more information becomes available to more people about nutrition and exercise, the natural functions of the body—expressed in movement—inspire the design of anything from running shoes to office furniture.

Often discussed as if it were a completely new invention, the organically derived design has been evolving for at least a century. It was in the 1850s that American engineers, sensing the new rhythms of a rapidly mechanizing society, began in earnest to explore movement. When they combined the rocking chair with the revolving chair, they ushered in a new era of sitting.

The result was a piece of furniture that could move with the body and flex its frame with the person's muscles. The support and resistance provided by such chairs were increasingly recognized as healthful exercise for the body at rest. Although originally intended for domestic use, the mobile chair caught on in the office. Here it gave a new expression to the alert readiness required in a highly competitive business setting.

Sitting down to work was a fact of modern life by the 1950s. Corporations, looking to house their growing "white collar" work force, were drawn to enormous and anonymous containers. These elaborations of 1920s avant-garde architectural ideas continued to promise efficiencies in construction and operation achieved by standardized elements. The resulting offices have changed the varied landscape into a uniform forest of steel, concrete, and glass. These transparent structures, with their floors seemingly hovering in mid air, announced the aesthetic necessity for light-weight, resilient, and gravity-defying furniture.

The old fashioned mobile chair was adapted to the various status requirements of the modern office. Its slimmed-down, vinyl-covered version squeaked under the worker; while its highly padded, leather-tufted incarnation tilted and swiveled authoritatively under the executive.

The board members and the visitors to the executive floors were often treated to a new elegance in furnishings in the form of pleasantly vibrating chairs—many of them made after the 1920s and 1930s designs of avant-garde architects. These resilient chairs (usually made of steel, sometimes plywood) remain in use today and continue to inspire new generations of designs.

The now familiar sling seat and back, originally made of thin membranes of fabric or leather, which were tautly stretched on the frames, appear in current designs as plastics, metal fabrics, and sheet metal. While in some cases the original idea of resilience is refined by the new elasticity of the nearly

Photograph courtesy Krueger

Vertebra Systems chair

DESIGNERS: Emilio Ambasz and Giancarlo Piretti for OPENArK B.V.

MANUFACTURER: under license from OPENArK B.V. in the U.S.A., Krueger, Green Bay, Wisconsin

The manager's chair automatically adjusts to his body as he tilts forward, sits upright, relaxes, and tilts backward. The button under the seat releases the pneumatic device that regulates the chair's height.

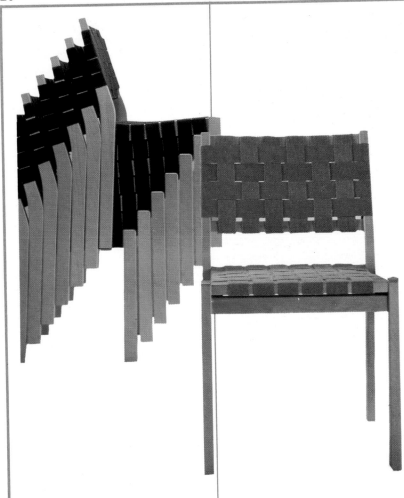

Aalto stacking chair

DESIGNER: Alvar Aalto

MANUFACTURER: Artek, Finland; International Contract Furnishings, New York, New York

Space saving, which became a major concern of modern life, is solved in this 1930 design of light-weight, linen webbed birch chairs, which stack when not needed. Their organic materials and curves reflect an on-going interest in objects that bear a trace of life.

transparent materials, others tend to rigidify into fascinating sculptures that attract the eye but have been known to eject the body.

At such moments of minor violence, the question of comfort naturally arises. Perhaps nothing illustrates the problem better than the experience of two people shopping for a chair. Even as the large, lumbering body of one has a tendency to slide out of a very attractive but stiff chair, the more compact, alert body of the other fits it perfectly. The slouching misery of one versus the buoyant pleasure of the other defines the basic rule of comfort: It's an individual thing.

Since many office chairs are purchased by interior designers, the issue of comfort is complicated even further. Add to the discrepancies of personalities and body sizes the social message a chair is expected to convey with its size and style, and it's a minor miracle that office workers find comfort at all.

The one hopeful development of recent years is the increasingly available information on body types and movements. The utilization of these facts, combined with the new technologies for molding materials, have contributed to the organically shaped chairs, which can be fine-tuned to many bodies. Height adjustments, movable parts, seamless upholstery, smoothly rolling wheels on stable bases are making it possible for each person to be "fitted" with his own chair.

Photograph courtesy ICF Inc.

Cesca armchair

DESIGNER: Marcel Breuer

MANUFACTURER: Knoll International, New York, New York

Expressing a major architectural innovation of the 1920s, which seemed to want to defy gravity by using thin, resilient materials to build cantilevered forms, this chair has become the most familiar modern design in its nearly six decades of production. Its continued popularity rests on a demand for light-weight and stable chairs that give a gently vibrating support to the active body.

Manufacturers are producing whole families of chairs from one basic design, and adapting these to the demands of corporations for "seating systems." The chairs are made to reinforce job descriptions, often disregarding body sizes. Although there's no law that states a secretary has to be a slim five-foot-two while the executive must be a burly six-footer, even the most democratically thought-out chairs pay homage to these preconceptions. The sizes and materials in one chair group may be as varied as a 19-inch-wide "task" chair, upholstered in "tough-wearing" synthetics and the 29-or-more-inch-wide "executive" chair in rare leathers and plush wools.

Regardless of the person's location on the corporate ladder, the work of the office continues to be conducted in a seated position. But the realities of work say something different. Even as machine operators are confined to their seats, occasionally rising to ask some disturbing questions about eye strain and birth defects; many executives deny their own freedom of movement. Their work as researchers, thinkers, planners, and socializers may be interpreted in furniture that supports daydreaming as well as the lumbar region. But such unbusinesslike postures seem to run counter to the etiquette of office behavior. A generation of business leaders, heirs to the hard-driving, energetic style of John F. Kennedy, seem to have forgotten his rocking chair.

Photograph courtesy Knoll

Ergon

DESIGNER:
Bill Stumpf

MANUFACTURER:
Herman Miller,
Zeeland, Michigan

Designer Bill Stumpf has identified three basic positions that an office worker's body is likely to take during the day. Here he demonstrates the "work intensive" posture, when the backrest and seat pan help tilt the body slightly forward while supporting it. In the "conversational" position, the body is stabilized while the chair's armrests allow the legs to be draped over the side and the arms to move freely. No matter how accommodating a chair is, long term sitting is tiring. In the "relaxation/stretching" position the chair's back-tilt mechanism lets Stumpf stretch his body and flex his arms and legs.

In 1976, before "user friendly" products were being cataloged, those who saw the first Ergon chairs were commenting on how "friendly" they were. The way we see a chair influences our feelings about it, even after we've used it for a while; our emotional reactions seem to have been designed into this chair.

Beyond appearances, the chairs give support to many types of bodies, in many of the postures that each of these individuals may decide to assume during the workday. Thus the name Ergon, which is short for "ergonomic," the scientific term usually used to describe the study of the body at work.

In addition to their cushioned and rounded surfaces, smoothly rolling casters, firm but easy tilts and swivels, the chairs work to stabilize the lower body and angle the pelvis slightly forward, which is the "correct spinal curvature."

Beyond the spine, the next main concern of action chair designers is the body's extremities. A relatively short seat pan prevents the chair's front edge from cutting into the back of the sitter's legs.

The chubby armrests, in addition to supporting elbows and arms when required, show the kind of sensitive understanding of "users" that designers like to talk about, but rarely achieve. Because the armrests are short, the chairs can be pulled up to the desk for those intense moments of concentration. In

Photographs courtesy Herman Miller

The "executive chair's" high back is designed to give extra support for conversational postures. Its compression-spring back tilt mechanism is calibrated to work with bodies weighing anywhere from 90 to 235 pounds.

addition, their curve and location on the chair allow free body movement sideways, when in the discursive posture the legs and arms move expressively. In this "side mount" position, the person's back can rest on the chair's arm, while the chair's back cools off.

Like the many action chairs inspired by Ergon, its operating mechanisms offer an opportunity to fine tune it to a person. Levers activate adjustments to the backrest's tension and height. The height can be altered simply by rotating the empty chair. For those who like more technology and a feeling of extra cushioning when they sit down, the pneumatic device built into the shaft of the base requires a simple coordination of body and hand movements.

In keeping with marketing trends, which label furniture according to job titles, this decidedly democratic chair also has "executive, management, operational, and secretarial" versions, as well as a drafting stool and a lounge chair that has a "relaxed angle" and legs fitted with stable gliders.

Diffrient Seating

DESIGNER: Niels Diffrient

MANUFACTURER: Knoll International, New York, New York

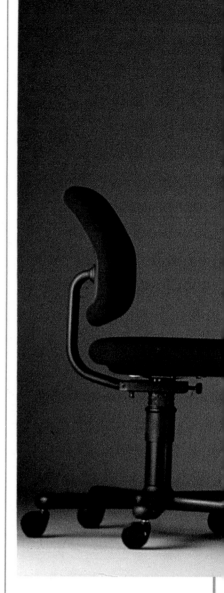

As an industrial designer Niels Diffrient has been at the forefront of what some call the scientific approach to design. His work is based on carefully gathered information about body measurements and movements. He prefers to call this process "human factors" study, a somewhat more accessible term than "ergonomics." His three decades of observing and cataloging body movements prompts him to say that "human

factors is design. You don't fight it. If you go with the information, you'll find it's telling you what the form can be."

Applying these thoughts to the problem of designing a comfortable chair—which by definition gives good support to the spine, neck, head, thighs, and buttocks—Diffrient has devised a shape that closely resembles the seated body. The chair's gently angled back support, in conjunction with the

shallow scoop of the seat, gives the spine that slightly concave contour that puts the least amount of stress on it. But Diffrient is the first to admit that because seating is basically an "unnatural" human position, "the best chair is really a bed, because the load of your body weight is spread out over the largest possible area."

But office tradition dictates the seated position, and this family of chairs conforms to that

rule. While none of the models can be called luxurious or overtly status-reinforcing, the people who manage get wider and larger chairs than the machine operators.

The materials used take into consideration the many adversities a chair will encounter in highly fluid business environments. The shells are made of stamped steel to which a dark brown paint is fused. This process, as well as the soft plastisol

Feet planted firmly on the floor, designer Niels Diffrient tilts back in his "advanced management armchair," which he has adjusted to his own height.

material that covers the chair's arms and legs, is meant to hide knicks and bruises to the chairs, just as the rounded edges protect the human body.

Playing a major part in the chair's "human engineered" appearance is the seamless upholstery, which is reminiscent of the elegant way our skin keeps our own bodies neat. One piece of fabric is molded to a polyurethane foam cushion, which is anchored to the steel shell. When reupholstery is required, the assembly is simply removed and replaced by a new one.

The pneumatic cylinder, concealed inside the urethane bellows under the seat, can move the seat up or down within a three-inch range. The control lever for this operation is under the arm or in the armless chairs under the seat; as is the lever that regulates the chair's tilt.

Vertebra® Seating System

DESIGNERS: Emilio Ambasz and Giancarlo Piretti for OPENArK B.V.

MANUFACTURER: under license from OPENArK B.V. in the U.S.A., Krueger, Green Bay, Wisconsin

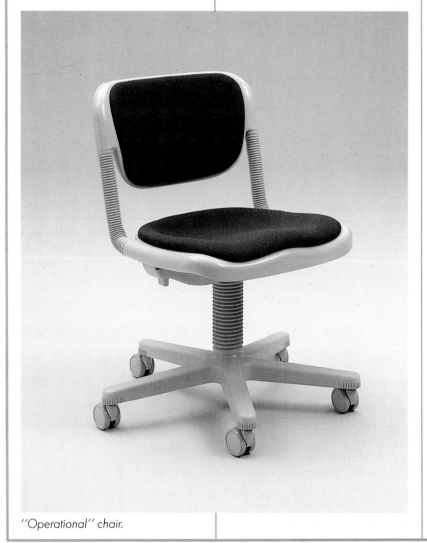

''Operational'' chair.

''Manager's'' chair.

Photographs and drawings courtesy Krueger

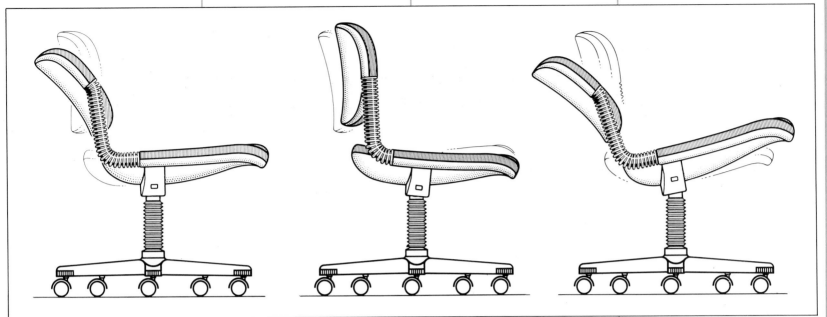

The "manager's" chair's three active positions: relax (left), tilt forward (middle), tilt backward (right).

Like the healthy body's nervous system, which functions without any outside adjustments, so the internal workings of Vertebra® respond to the sitting person's movements. Sit up: The chair assumes an upright position. Tilt forward: The seat tilts downward. Lean back: The seat slides forward while the backrest tilts backward.

As with other families of chairs, this one also gives most favored treatment to the executives. Their chairs are wider, have a more daring, deeper tilt, and thicker, more luxurious cushions, with or without quilting, than the less celebrated models. The executive can also exercise his or her shoulders by pressing back on the extra-high, double-jointed backrest.

A soft-feeling synthetic rubber bellows hides the pneumatic height control inside the shaft of the base. The chair's only control knob is on those models that have this device. Others are adjusted by simply rotating the empty chair.

The bellows also covers the sinewy armrests, which are actually curved-forward extensions of the chair's back support. This elegant solution, with its economy of line and textural harmony, makes the bellows-armed chairs in the group especially attractive.

The obligatory five-toed foot, made of steel, is softened by self-skinning urethane colors of sand, umber, or black.

In addition to providing seating for offices, the collection adapts comfortably to auditoriums, lecture halls, public waiting rooms, and other places where large numbers of people sit together.

Helena

DESIGNER:
Niels Diffrient

MANUFACTURER:
Sunar, Waterloo,
Ontario

In 1982 large numbers of people—most of whom already had experienced responsive chairs in their offices—were told by *Time* magazine what a really good chair is about, when the magazine singled out Helena as one of the ten best-designed objects of the year. What makes the chair so good is best explained by industrial designer Don Albinson, who is recognized for his adjustable chair designs.

"It looks like it does what it's supposed to do, and it really does it well. It works smoothly, has good motion, the back goes a long way, the seat moves little so your feet don't get lifted, it's not too hard or soft, it's adjustable, and as an office chair it's the antithesis of the sharp-edged, anti-personal chairs of the 1950s that seemed more to accommodate cardboard cartons than people."

The chair's frame is built on an axle, which moves the armpiece and the back support together. A small black box, clearly visible under the seat, contains all the mechanisms. The seat is a stamped steel pan, sandwiched inside a smoothly upholstered cushion. It carries the load of the axle, which attaches to it with strong nylon bearings. The currently popular five-toed foot (four toes used to be enough only a few years ago) is made of molded plastic. Double casters on each toe give this chair ten small wheels on which it is able to roll both smoothly and securely.

In addition to explaining his work as a fight against "herneated disks" with the aid of "human engineering," the designer also recognizes the emotional appeal of a product: It starts "when you first see it in an advertisement, how you use it, how it wears over time, how you maintain it, how your friends look upon you as owning it."

Photograph courtesy Sunar

Each member of this family of chairs has a back cushion that feels as if it were glued to the sitter's back.

Dorsal®

DESIGNERS:
Emilio Ambasz
and
Giancarlo Piretti
for OPENArK B.V.

MANUFACTURER:
under exclusive license
from OPENArK B.V. in
the U.S.A., Krueger,
Green Bay, Wisconsin

The jurors of *Industrial Design* magazine's Design Review for 1983 recognized Dorsal® for its "low cost, simplicity, and ingenious use of material," but withheld the award. They called its aesthetics "questionable," citing the chair's "awkward base and uncoordinated upholstery, and the shape of the legs and their disruptive scale in relation to the seat."

The judgment may be a reflection of the current tension between designers who use increasingly available data on the workings of the human body—which often leads them to talk like orthopedists and research scientists—and the traditional designers whose main concern is aesthetics.

Dorsal® is an excellent amalgam of science and design, making life a little more pleasant for large numbers of people, even beyond the office. It brings "ergonomic principles" into public areas where people have already become used to "organic" fiberglass bucket seats, Charles Eames's far-reaching contribution to the way we sit. Ambasz and Piretti's concern with body movement expands on Eames's organic ideal. The movement of the chair not only aids blood circulation, but exercises the muscles, as well as keeping the mind alert.

The chair's body is made of thermoplastic, by a process called injection molding, which twenty years ago gave new life to the Italian furniture industry. Except for the textured area in the pocket that is formed by the seat saddle and the backrest, the chair is a sleek, slim shell, supported by steel legs, which

Time-lapse photograph shows the operational chair in action: tilt forward, sit up, relax.

"Operational" chairs have armed and armless versions.

are coated with a shiny, electrostatically bonded paint.

"Mass seating" includes chairs that stack for storage or attach to steel frames in tandem. The seats on these chairs remain fixed as the backrests respond to the sitter's movement.

The "operational" and "managerial" versions follow the forward tilting ("work intensive") movement of the body, by tilting downward together. This position can be locked in place, as can the height adjustments, which are made by a pneumatic cylinder in the stem of the base.

The backrest is joined to the bucket of the seat by a steel hinge, which contains a spring. The resilient action of the plastic bellows, which hide these hinges, is a small detail that can delight scientists and aestheticians alike.

Vitraflex chairs

DESIGNER: Wolfgang Muller-Deisig

MANUFACTURER: Vitra GmbH, Germany; Herman Miller, Zeeland, Michigan

The hinged back is designed to move with the upper body. It is joined to the stationary lower back support, which forms the bucket of the seat.

Flexturn chair

DESIGNER: Gerd Lange

MANUFACTURER: Beylerian, New York, New York

Seat and back are joined together by a flexible nylon sleeve, which attaches to the bentwood or steel tubing that round out the chair's edges.

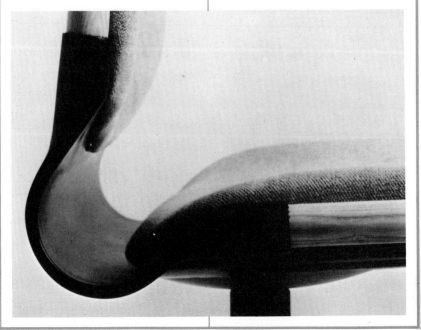

Top photograph courtesy Herman Miller

Bottom photograph courtesy Beylerian

Serie 6600 chair

DESIGNER: Jorgen Kastholm

MANUFACTURER: Kusch & Co., Germany; Harvey Probber, Fall River, Massachussetts

Seat and back adjust automatically and independently of one another when the body moves. The knob in the back turns to adjust to the back height; the bracket under the seat operates the chair's pneumatic lift.

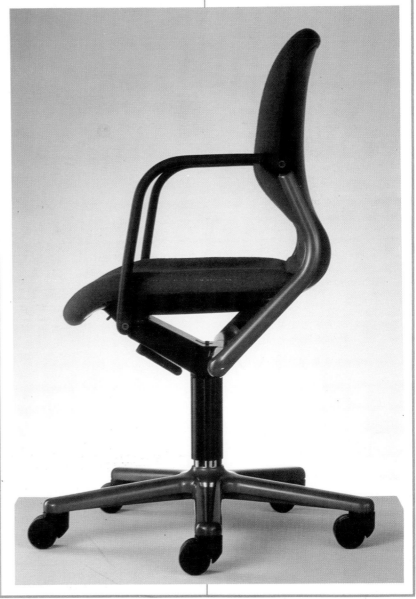

Wilkhahn chair

DESIGNERS: Klaus Franck and Werner Sauer

MANUFACTURER: Wilkhahn GmbH, Germany; Vecta Contract, Grand Prairie, Texas

Spring tension between three points of the frame works in unison with the chair's suspension system. The pivot point for tilting is at the front edge of the seat; gravity is centered at the central pivot; while the lumbar region's pivot is in the backrest.

Top photograph courtesy Harvey Probber

Bottom photograph courtesy Vecta

Kinetics chair

DESIGNER: Paolo Favaretto

MANUFACTURER: Kinetics Furniture,
Rexdale, Ontario

*Highly organic contours and details
are achieved by a process called
injection molding, which forms plastic
materials into the chair's smoothly
curving parts.*

Top and bottom left photographs courtesy Kinetics

Stephens executive chair

DESIGNER: William Stephens

MANUFACTURER: Knoll International, New York, New York

The already commodious seating area can be made even larger by simple adjustments to the chair's back and its arms. Its height can be raised or lowered 2 ½ inches by rotating the empty chair. The firm but softly rounded cushions are achieved by molding foam around plywood inserts.

Montara executive seating

DESIGNER: Brian Kane

MANUFACTURER: Metropolitan Furniture Corp., South San Francisco, California

Pre-sewn covers provide the option of easy reupholstery at a time when pastel colors are becoming popular in office decoration.

Center photograph courtesy Metropolitan Furniture Corp.

Top photograph courtesy Knoll

Wilkhahn 61 armchair

DESIGNERS: Moll/Piehl

MANUFACTURER: Wilkhahn GmbH, Germany; Vecta Contract, Grand Prairie, Texas

The tailored leather hides a supple, polyurethane foam and fiberfill core inside a three-piece cushion, which snap-fastens to the frame and is easily removed for replacement. The metal arms are warmed to the touch by tightly fitting sleeves of leather.

Carlos Riart chair

DESIGNER: Carlos Riart

MANUFACTURER: Knoll International, New York, New York

A well-balanced rocking chair with generous upholstery and a relaxed pitch can turn movement into a gentle exercise of leg and foot muscles. The simple frame is accented by an abstract decoration: mother of pearl inlays on the dark, ebony and Brazilian amaranth frame; ebony inlays on the light, holly frame.

Photograph courtesy Vecta

Photograph courtesy Knoll

The pension chair

DESIGNER: Alvar Aalto

MANUFACTURER: Artek, Finland; International Contract Furnishings, New York, New York

The body is cradled in gentle motion by the linen-webbed, one-piece seat and back, which is cantilevered from a laminated birch frame. Although this design was put into production in 1946, it represents nearly twenty years of experimentation with laminating Finnish birch for furniture to resemble in resilience and grace the famous skis made from the same.

Tulip chair

DESIGNER: Eero Saarinen

MANUFACTURER: Knoll International, New York, New York

Fiberglass-reinforced plastic is molded into the cooly sensuous shape of the seat's shell, which rotates on a cast aluminum stem. Nearly twenty years after they were designed, the chair and its companion table continue to represent "futuristic" design, sometimes appearing in films and advertisements for personal computers.

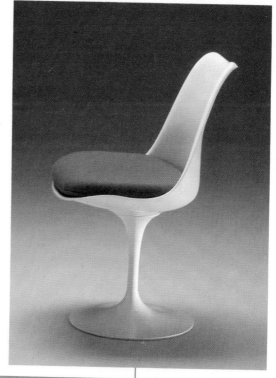

Herbst side chair

DESIGNER: Rene Herbst

MANUFACTURER: Ecart International, France; Furniture of the Twentieth Century, New York, New York

In 1928, long before it was fashionable to call industrial materials "high tech," this chair was made with automotive tension straps. The reproductions have the same, springy seats and backs strung between welded tubular steel frames.

Mezzadro chair

DESIGNERS: Achille and Piergiancomo Castiglioni

MANUFACTURER: Zanotta, Italy; International Contract Furnishings, New York, New York

The metal saddle that put American farm machine operators of the 1850s on a cushion of air has inspired much modern design with its gravity-defying hovering and resilient strength. A 1950s design in wood, chromed steel, and enameled metal recalls the historical antecedent with literal humor.

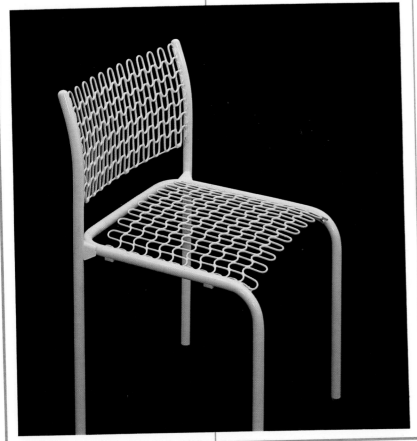

Sof-Tech stacking chair

DESIGNER: David Rowland

MANUFACTURER: Thonet, York, Pennsylvania

The modern fascination with ordinary industrial materials, which may be transformed into other uses, has been occupying this designer since the 1950s. Success came in 1979 when he coated steel-wire furniture springs with a PVC plastisol that flattens them, holds them in alignment, and allows them to stretch slightly under the sitter's weight. The light-weight, tubular-steel framed chairs stack in a compact space.

Bottom left photograph courtesy Thonet

Top left photograph courtesy Furniture of the Twentieth Century

Bertoia chair

DESIGNER: Harry Bertoia

MANUFACTURER: Knoll International, New York, New York

Showing the early 1950s occupation with organic forms and resilient but strong materials, welded wire is bent to make the basket and sled base of this chair. It has become a perennial favorite, both indoors and out.

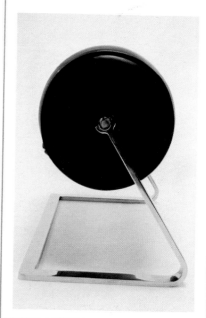

1059 footrest

DESIGNER: Ward Bennett

MANUFACTURER: Brickel Associates, New York, New York

The footrest, once a standard piece of library furniture, is rarely seen in offices; although the physical need to elevate the feet remains. An upholstered bolster, raised 13 inches in the air by a bent stainless steel rod, revives a considerate tradition.

Bottom center photograph courtesy ICF Inc.   Top photograph courtesy Knoll   Bottom right photographs courtesy Brickel

The spaghetti group

DESIGNER: Giandomenico Belotti

MANUFACTURER: International Contract Furnishings, New York, New York

Soft, highly tactile PVC strings wind around the slim, tubular steel frames, providing pleasantly resilient seating.

Bumper chair

DESIGNER: Brian Kane

MANUFACTURER: Metropolitan Furniture Corp., South San Francisco, California

Tubular steel frames are softened considerably with the addition of rubber sleeves, which may be pulled off for replacement. The seats, also replaceable, are a trim cushion or a waferlike stained wood.

Bottom photograph courtesy Metropolitan Furniture Corp.

Top photograph courtesy ICF Inc.

Penelope chair

DESIGNER: Charles Pollock

MANUFACTURER: Castelli, New York, New York

A new mastery of modern materials may be seen in the sinewy curves of a tempered steel rod (18 feet long), which bends in one continuing, complex line to form the support structure of a wire-net seating shell.

Brno armchair

DESIGNER: Ludwig Mies van der Rohe

MANUFACTURER: Knoll International, New York, New York

Flat stainless steel is bent to give a springy support to the hovering upholstery. This 1930 design for a central-European home has become a favorite chair in multinational board rooms.

Bottom photograph courtesy Knoll

Top photograph courtesy Castelli

Bitsch seating

DESIGNER: Hans Ulrich Bitsch

MANUFACTURER: Kusch & Co.,
Germany; Harvey Probber, Fall River,
Massachusetts

*The on-going search for a material
that is thinner and stronger than
others—as well as fire and water
resistant—has led to the use of a
stainless steel fabric to build a
completely metal chair. These
iridescent membranes are stretched
under tension to form the chair's seat
and back, fastened invisibly to its
suspension frame. "A computerized
welding robot makes the thirty metal-
to-metal connections required to
produce one of these chairs,"
according to the manufacturer.
Canvas seats in many colors, tandem
arrangements, and armed versions
complete this "seating system."*

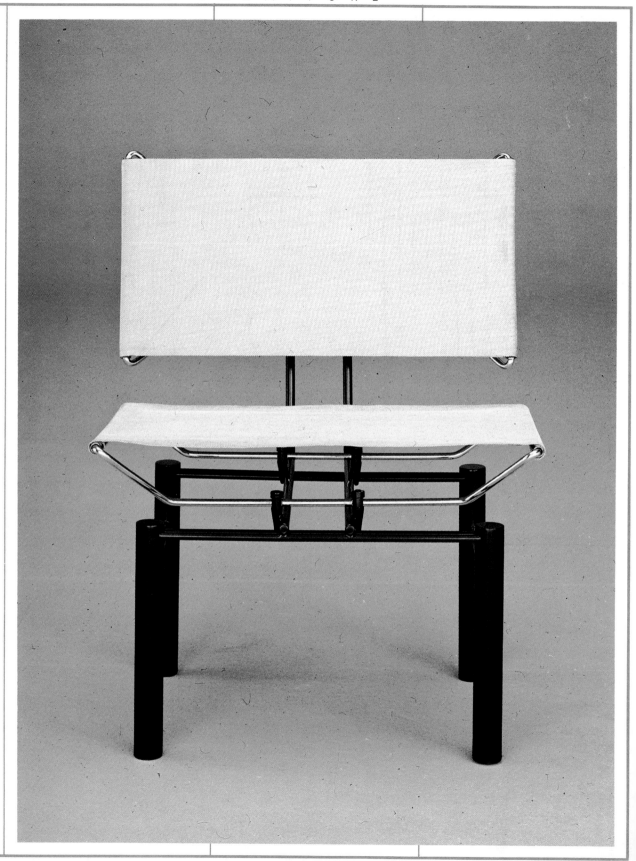

Photographs courtesy Harvey Probber

LC1 sling chair

DESIGNERS: LeCorbusier, Pierre Jeanneret, Charlotte Perriand

MANUFACTURER: Cassina, Italy; Atelier International, New York, New York

Slings that form the arms (leather), the seat, and the pivoting back (canvas) become tautly stretched membranes between polished chrome-plated steel tubes. The 1928 design continues to delight visual sensibilities while challenging ideas of comfort.

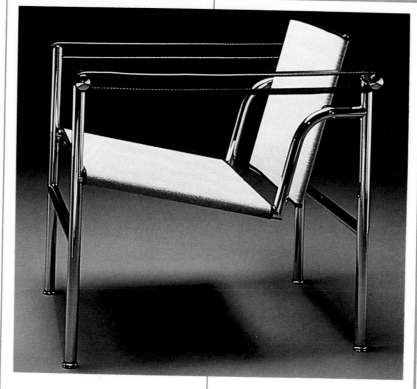

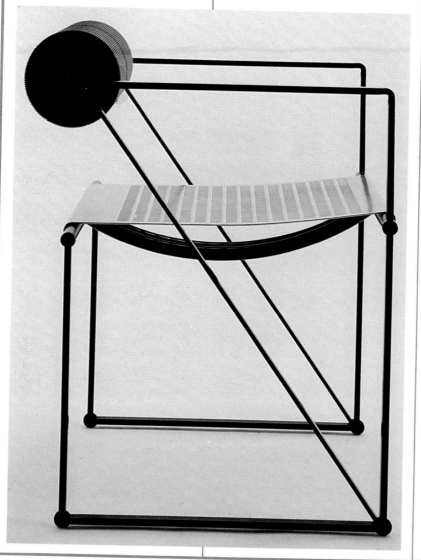

The Seconda armchair

DESIGNER: Mario Botta

MANUFACTURER: International Contract Furnishings, New York, New York

Received enthusiastically as the "first important object to emerge out of the rationalist movement," this 1982 design continues the search for industrially produced materials that seem to dematerialize in their thinness and transparency. Fine-gauge tubular steel frame, perforated sheet metal seat, polyurethane cylinders that rotate around the backrest, and small, circular plastic glides are intellectually satisfying design details that compose a chair of contestable comfort.

Bottom photograph courtesy ICF Inc.

Top photograph courtesy Atelier International

Portable Wood Chairs

Even as the new humanoid office chair works for the healthy comfort of the physical body, the familiar wood chair can strengthen the soul at moments of great transition and uncertainty. It can be a subtle reminder of nature's resilience and endurance. It can signify that elusive but reassuring continuum between the past and the future. It can please the senses with its warm, organic material, which needs the hand to shape its form, and which in turn invites the touch of another hand.

It is not surprising that many of the wood chairs we find attractive today were first made or inspired by the designs of this century's early years. As that generation tried to cope with its leap into mechanization, so we face computerization.

Although we now know that "going back to nature" is only a dream; our need to combine the organic with the technologies we've devised is nonetheless real.

The incessant talk of "humanizing" the office reflects a concern for this need. The most successful attempts are those that treat people as creatures of nature who require unprocessed sunshine and air, and who are presumed to be capable of making judgments about how they do their best work.

Traditional pieces of furniture, like the "pull-up" chair with arms that can be grasped and fondled or the little wooden stool that allows the sitter to face in any direction, continue to serve us well into a new age.

Riemerschmid armchair

DESIGNER: Richard Riemerschmid

MANUFACTURER: Larsen Furniture, New York, New York

Like the living tree which preceded it, the solid beechwood frame has an animated, organic presence. Designed in 1899 for a Dresden music room, the chair is now back in production, with minor adjustments that make it wider and deeper than the original.

The White Chair

DESIGNER: Eliel Saarinen

MANUFACTURER: International Contract Furnishings, New York, New York

Designed in 1902 for Hvittrask (white lake), the architect's home, now a museum on a romantic lakeside outside of Helsinki, the current reproduction revives Finnish Jugendstil, a charming celebration of nature and its forms.

Left photograph courtesy Larsen Furniture

Fledermaus spindle-back chair

DESIGNER: Josef Hoffmann

MANUFACTURER: International Contract Furnishings, New York, New York

Small and somewhat stiff, the beechwood chair has none of the frills but all the charm of Vienna café society at the turn of the century. With its companion pieces (table, settee, rocking chair), the chair's current popularity speaks to our nostalgia for places like the Fledermaus Café for which it was designed in 1909.

Center and above photographs courtesy ICF Inc.

D.S.4 lounge chair

DESIGNER: Charles Rennie Mackintosh

MANUFACTURER: Cassina, Italy; Atelier International, New York, New York

An intellectualized version of the Art Nouveau style, which is more widely known for its florid curves, the ebonized ashwood chair, contrary to its original design date of 1918, remains remarkably fresh today. A seagrass seat and mother of pearl inlays at its crown detail a love of nature.

Aalto armchair

DESIGNER: Alvar Aalto

MANUFACTURER: Artek, Finland; International Contract Furnishings, New York, New York

Since 1947, when it was designed, this solid beech and rattan chair has been continuously in production. Its generous size, light weight, pleasing curves, and subtle texture are just some reasons for its popularity.

Bottom photograph courtesy ICF Inc.

Top photograph courtesy Atelier International

University chair

DESIGNER: Ward Bennett

MANUFACTURER: Brickel Associates, New York, New York

No upholstery is needed to make this hardwood chair comfortable. Its sloped, contoured back and seat, along with its gently curving arms have been inviting sitters since 1978 when it was designed for the LBJ Library at the University of Texas.

Gina armchair

DESIGNER: Bern Makulik

MANUFACTURER: Stendig International, New York, New York

A small detail—the flaring out of its arms—gives a "stylish" quality to the solid beech frame. Its finish—matte or glossy natural, light walnut, black, or red—emphasizes the memorable silhouette.

Bottom photograph courtesy Stendig

Top photographs courtesy Brickel

711 folding chair

DESIGNER: Michael Kirkpatrick

MANUFACTURER: CI Designs, Medford, Massachusetts

For offices long on meetings but short on space, the ashwood folding chair reduces to a mere 2½-inch frame for compact storage.

Kita armchair

DESIGNER: Toshiyuki Kita

MANUFACTURER: Stendig International, New York, New York

Red, blue, black, pale gray, pale green, and pale pink, in addition to the natural color of solid beech, accent the delicate lines of this slim chair.

Top photograph courtesy CI Designs

Bottom photograph courtesy Stendig

Acorn chairs

DESIGNERS: Lella and Massimo Vignelli

MANUFACTURER: Sunar, Waterloo, Ontario

In less sensitive hands, right-angled motifs could be all edges. But here they're softened by the smooth turnings of the arms, legs, and contoured back panel. Seats are cane, cushion, or a sling of leather or fabric.

Photograph courtesy Sunar

Andover armchair

DESIGNER: Davis Allen

MANUFACTURER: Stendig International, New York, New York

A continuously curving beechwood rail organizes the contoured spindles of the chair's back and its upright arms. Its "clean-cut" appearance, generously high back and cushioned seat, accented by its attractive colors—from black to burgundy— could promote this chair into "a new American classic," as some have suggested.

Continuum seating

DESIGNER: Warren Snodgrass

MANUFACTURER: Stow/Davis, Grand Rapids, Michigan

The solid white oak or American black walnut chairs with French-seamed upholstery are designed to be stacked in groups of six when not needed.

Top photograph courtesy Stendig

Bottom photographs courtesy Stow/Davis

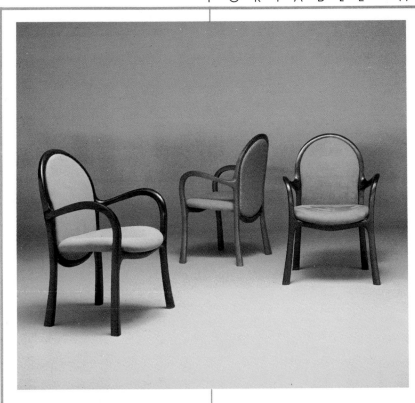

Sculpted chair

DESIGNER: Thomas Lamb

MANUFACTURER: Nienkamper, Toronto, Ontario

The uninhibited curves of the chairs' solid cherry or ash frames express a new freedom in styling, aided by a memory for organic forms.

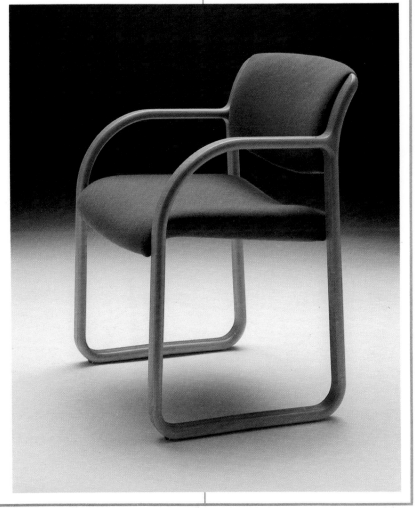

Snodgrass chair

DESIGNER: Warren Snodgrass

MANUFACTURER: Steelcase, Grand Rapids, Michigan

Originally designed as a steel chair, the same curved frame has been adapted to a warmed-up version in wood.

Top photograph courtesy Nienkamper   Bottom photograph courtesy Steelcase

Fan-legged stools

DESIGNER: Alvar Aalto

MANUFACTURER: Artek, Finland;
International Contract Furnishings,
New York, New York

Throughout his productive career, the architect experimented with sensually curving organic forms, such as the fan-shaped legs of stools and tables, which were first produced of natural birch in 1954.

Meier stool

DESIGNER: Richard Meier

MANUFACTURER: Knoll
International, New York, New York

Made by traditional mortise and tenon construction, the low (15¼-inch) and high (27½-inch) maple stools have hand-rubbed finishes of black or white lacquer-urethane or low-sheen vinyl to protect the natural wood. The architect's personal mark is imprinted on each piece.

Photograph courtesy Knoll

Center photograph courtesy ICF Inc.

Austrian Postal Savings Bank Stool

DESIGNER: Otto Wagner

MANUFACTURER: Thonet, York, Pennsylvania

The same manufacturer who produced the original stools when they were designed in 1903 is now making the reproductions from steam-bent American ash, which support a molded-plywood top at 18½ inches.

Top photograph courtesy Thonet

Movable Tables

When writing was the way people communicated information, tables and desks were impressively scaled and elaborately detailed objects. Now that writing can be done on machines, the table has become an object of transition. It is asked to support equipment, charts, papers, cups, ashtrays, as well as the hand that writes. It's pressed into service, on demand, to put a safe distance between people and then assume an auxiliary position when the confrontation is over. Tables on wheels, tables that rotate, tables that can be taken apart, all express the mobility of the modern office worker.

G.S.A. table

DESIGNER: Charles Rennie
Mackintosh

MANUFACTURER: Cassina, Italy;
Atelier International, New York,
New York

Designed in 1900 as a meeting table for the Board of Governors of the Glasgow School of Art, the 72-inch-diameter ash table's central portion rotates and can be raised 1 inch higher than its edge. Although the current reproduction remains faithful to the original design, the nylon wheels, which give a smooth rotation to the top, are a welcome innovation. Each table is accompanied by its own "identity card," which describes its history and construction.

Photograph courtesy Atelier International

Belschner table group

DESIGNER: Andrew Belschner

MANUFACTURER: Metropolitan Furniture Corp., South San Francisco, California

"Seafoam," "elephant," and "paper bag" are some of the twenty-one highly decorative colors listed by the manufacturer for their collection of high and low tables. The geometric structures, made of light-weight particle board, are finished by a cast polyester resin process, which makes multiple color combinations possible. The red table, for instance, coordinates "coral" with "flesh."

Hoffmann nesting tables

DESIGNER: Josef Hoffmann

MANUFACTURER: International Contract Furnishings, New York, New York

Designed in 1905 to support the various paraphernalia of turn-of-the-century entertainments in a Viennese home, the small tables that fit into a compact unit are also important pieces of furniture in modern offices where space is costly and often ungenerous. Three tables nest under the 27½-inch-high and 19¾-inch-wide unit. They are made of ash, in natural or limed black-stain finishes.

Bottom photographs courtesy ICF Inc.

Top photograph courtesy Metropolitan Furniture Corp.

Schröder 1 table

DESIGNER: Gerrit T. Rietveld

MANUFACTURER: Cassina, Italy;
Atelier International, New York,
New York

*Until recently, the small end table,
which was designed for the famous
Schröder house in Utrecht, Holland,
in 1918, was known and much
admired only by artists and historians.
Now it is being made, according to
the original specifications, from five
pieces of wood, each of which is
given a strong identity by its own
color: red, blue, black, white, and
yellow. Each table is stamped by the
manufacturer with a serial number in
the order of production.*

de Menil table

DESIGNERS: Charles Gwathmey
and Robert Siegel

MANUFACTURER: International
Contract Furnishings, New York,
New York

*While many architects' furniture
designs wait decades to be
appreciated and revived by
manufacturers who perceive a market
for them, Gwathmey Siegel's tables
for the de Menil house went into
production in 1983, just as the Long
Island mansion was completed and
widely publicized. Designed to go
with the owner's important collection
of furniture from Vienna, made in the
beginning of this century, these tables
show that same restraint of
decoration, which distinguishes the
best of that Austrian furniture. The
inlay pattern of the top inscribes the
shape of the support; thus the
decoration is seen as a natural
outcome of the design, not an added
frill, as proponents of the "rationalist"
movement like to point out.*

Top photograph courtesy Atelier International

D'Urso tables

DESIGNER: Joseph Paul D'Urso

MANUFACTURER: Knoll
International, New York, New York

The same slimmed-down and smoothed-out mobility that is designed into office chairs also identifies a collection of tables with many different top options, including squares, circles, and racetracks; made of wood veneers, laminates, or stone. The trim steel legs roll on small casters.

Lucia Mercer tables

DESIGNER: Lucia Mercer

MANUFACTURER: Knoll
International, New York, New York

Stone honed to a fine finish is made into low tables that look wonderfully at ease indoors as well as outdoors. True to her organic materials, the sculptor has chosen these angled shapes because they remind her of "trees blowing in the wind." Stones with romantic names like Canadian black onyx, Dakota mahogany, and gem mist are made into two kinds of tables. One has an elliptical top, which cantilevers from a slanted base. The other is simply a tilting trunk (15 inches high and 13 inches in diameter), which, when arranged in groups, inevitably prompts people to use them as stools.

Top left and bottom photographs courtesy Knoll

Capsule conference table

DESIGNER: Ward Bennett

MANUFACTURER: Brickel Associates, New York, New York

The specialized design of the operating table is adapted to a more general use for offices. The table's sturdy, stainless steel scaffold has rails that can be grasped by the hand and support the foot. It rolls on 5-inch rubber wheels; its top is protected from stains by a polyurethane enamel finish.

Top photograph courtesy Brickel

Lounge Seating

Some seating designs are clearly successful expressions of the modern concern with combining standardized parts into unique groupings. Their light-weight forms seem to ride a cushion of air or mold to the shape of a room. They provide attractive and utilitarian seating for many people comfortably.

It is no coincidence that the best of these modular seating groups—a new name for the old sofa, which can now extend into infinity—were designed during the 1970s when furniture made of panels, posts, and containers was being assembled in a growing number of open plan offices. Many of those installations are now trying to solve problems brought on by the new openness with its shared spaces, deadly repetitiveness, and hard-to-understand traffic patterns.

The call to "humanize" the office has become the Muzak of design professionals. While many merely repeat its ambiguous message, others try to understand it by decreasing the scale: Instead of dreaming of an infinity of solutions from simple modules, they're going back to the old, familiar pieces of furniture: the sofa, the settee, and the club chair. They add special stitching to the upholstery, emphasize the beauty of inlaid woods, and celebrate the richness of materials. Some of the new lounge furniture looks as if it's meant to be an oasis of sensual pleasures that waits at the edges of the "work stations" to revitalize bodies and eyes exhausted by millions of tiny electronic messages.

Photograph courtesy Herman Miller

Wilkes modular sofa group

DESIGNER: Ray Wilkes

MANUFACTURER: Herman Miller, Zeeland, Michigan

Soft-looking but firm-sitting blocks of foam can be combined into individual seating arrangements. The blocks are made by a process called cold cured polyurethane injection foam molding, which is what gives each module its perfectly formed, seamless, rounded appearance. Looking like a very fine, white sponge, the polyurethane foam is molded around an integral structure of plywood sheets joined by steel armatures. This is done to add extra support to the backs of the "sofa." A touchable, tailored upholstery material stretches over the foam blocks, just like skin on flesh. A tubular steel frame supports the rows of seats, which can be alternated with tables that are made on the same module as the foam blocks. The total effect is that of a cushion, with individually assigned seats, hovering invitingly above the ground.

Circolo and Rotonda

DESIGNERS: Lella and Massimo Vignelli

MANUFACTURER: Sunar, Waterloo, Ontario

Unabashedly luxurious, the Circolo seating group—armchair, settee, and sofa—has large, overstuffed bolsters, which encircle its gently rounded supports of veneered or lacquered shells. The wrinkles in the soft leather promise comfort and tactile delights. The Rotonda chair—its lightness and mobility confirmed by its small wheels—is simply an upholstered panel that supports the seat and curves to form the base and fanciful arms. The new delight in craftsmanship and materials is expressed in Sunar's Kioto table by Gianfranco Frattini. Inspired by a traditional Japanese technique that intersects dark and light woods, this table forms a pattern of subtle contrasts, with light and shadow, and with open and closed spaces.

Photograph courtesy Sunar

D'Urso lounge seating

DESIGNER: Joseph Paul D'Urso

MANUFACTURER: Knoll International, New York, New York

Without mechanical adjustments, the 8-foot-long sofa can become a bed. When the large (22-inch-square) feather pillows—which cluster against the sofa's slim arm and back support—are removed, the uninterrupted, saddle-stitched seating surface becomes a comfortable sleeping surface. Return the pillows— at least ten of them—and sitters will instinctively build cozy, private nests for themselves. A rounded corner unit can be used to extend the sofa. The table, designed as a companion piece, has a hollow interior for magazines.

Diesis seating group

DESIGNERS: Antonio Citterio and Paolo Nava

MANUFACTURER: B & B America, New York, New York

A thin metal frame with leather-covered platforms and panels supports soft cushions of leather, stuffed with polyurethane foam and eiderdown. The group has been designed as a series of units, which can stand alone or be combined together. Included are one-armed (left or right) units like a chaise longue, an armchair, a two-seat or three-seat sofa; as well as two-armed units. The sofas can be formed to fit a corner by using tables designed for that purpose. Companion coffee tables have leather shelves under their clear or etched glass tops to hold magazines.

Bottom photograph courtesy B&B America

Top photograph courtesy Knoll

Photograph courtesy Herman Miller

Chadwick modular seating

DESIGNER: Don Chadwick

MANUFACTURER: Herman Miller, Zeeland, Michigan

Three basic shapes, one square and two wedges, can be combined into continuous seating that can update the traditional vocabulary of furnishings or create new, still unknown languages. A modern version of a Victorian circular sofa with a potted palm in its center is as easy to put together as a daring, serpentine curve that winds around columns and curls around corners. The square modules can be left alone as individual seats or combined.

Haus Koller chair

DESIGNER: Josef Hoffmann

MANUFACTURER: International Contract Furnishings, New York, New York

Exercising great restraint in decoration, the 1911-designed chair and its companion sofas—with their charming channel tufting accented by contrasting piping—have influenced various styles during the past eight decades, including Parisian Art Deco of the 1920s as well as the current decorative revivals, and continue to have a strong appeal of their own.

Photograph courtesy ICF Inc.

Baldwin sofa

DESIGNER: Ben Baldwin

MANUFACTURER: Larsen Furniture, New York, New York

The simple curve that adds a subtle twist to the sofa's arms and the upholstery with its tailored stitching call attention to themselves with a reassuring neatness.

U-chair

DESIGNER: Ward Bennett

MANUFACTURER: Brickel Associates, New York, New York

Even as the chair's softened U-shape encloses the sitter's body in a safe hug, its casters allow freedom of movement in space.

Bottom photograph courtesy Brickel

Top photograph courtesy Larsen Furniture

Torso

DESIGNER: Paolo Deganello

MANUFACTURER: Cassina, Italy; Atelier International, New York, New York

It is possible to sit, perch, stretch out, slouch, hang over, hide, and keep refreshments for mind and body close at hand, all in one piece of furniture. The free-form structure of the upholstery and table supported on tilting legs suggest motion: "A dialog between the animate body and inanimate form," some have said. In addition to the chaise longue, there's a sofa and an armchair.

Graves lounge group

DESIGNER: Michael Graves

MANUFACTURER: Sunar, Waterloo, Ontario

A new delight in decorative forms and details may be read in the bird's eye maple frames ornamented with ebony inlays and corner beads. The settee and chairs are tautly upholstered, with accents of decorative welting, in luxurious materials.

Photograph courtesy Atelier International

Photograph courtesy Sunar

Craftsmanship Revisited

Even as mechanization—now robotization—continues to reduce human hand movements to quick reflexes or eliminate them altogether from the process of production, the urge to use the hand to express the visions of the mind seems to gain new momentum. Never before in the annals of modernization—with its drive toward speed, numbers, and consumption—has there been such an interest in singular objects, often made meticulously for those who seek something of personal value and identification.

This can mean furniture made in limited editions by craftsmen under the supervision of a master; or furniture that protests against the sameness of industrial production with forms, colors, and decorations that are highly eccentric, therefore fashionable; or furniture that is meant to be sculpture but also happens to be utilitarian; or furniture that gathers together in its form and ornamentation familiar references from several historical styles; as well as furniture that might combine all of these impulses and yet accommodate the most sophisticated electronic devices.

Whether the attraction to the unique is an expression of a purely material delight, an homage to the past, a subtle social comment, an inside joke among the cognoscente, or merely a bid for the "affluent dollar," the fact remains that a whole range of new alternatives to mass-production furniture is currently available.

Some of the most interesting pieces are made by sculptors, artists, architects, and craftsmen whose involvement in the design of furniture continues a long tradition. Because of their relatively small size and utilitarian nature, household objects remain handy items for exploring ideas about form, balance, materials, and details. What gives these newest investigations their powerful presence is the interest of marketers who have a knack for exploiting the print media's hunger for "the new." Glossy magazines, Sunday supplements, and banner headlines in newspapers announce, with all the breathless excitement of a new romance, the "revival" of intriguing forms and virtuoso workmanship that can add new delight, security, and emotion to the seemingly empty moment.

A growing number of art galleries, showrooms, and exclusive shops cater to a public primed to purchase special pieces of furniture. There are also those shoppers, mostly professionals and business executives, already avid buyers of art objects, who want to be more involved in the creative process. Commissioning a desk or a set of chairs often gives them that opportunity.

A five-figure price tag on a desk seems to be perfectly acceptable to those who value exquisite combinations of exotic woods and precious metals. But what may seem like extravagant sums for a piece of furniture, do not announce the eminence of nouveau riche craftsmen. The very nature of their time-consuming work seems to preclude this growing body of serious professionals from the "time is money" standards that evaluate the work of other professionals. The time is yet to come when excellent craftspeople can afford to freely explore the nature of materials, methods, and forms, without having to take those commissions that require artists to copy themselves. When that time comes, there will truly be a new richness of choice in the marketplace.

Home office

DESIGNER: Johnny Grey

MANUFACTURER: Homeworks, London

Decorative details made by the traditional method of hand-turning wood are combined with machine-made parts and molded acrylic elements to produce a large collection. These "blur the distinction between the office and the study at home, by fulfilling the functions of the office within the aesthetics of the living room," writes the designer.

In addition to the traditional office needs for desks with "pedestal drawer" supports and "modesty panel" fronts, as well as tables in several sizes and heights, attention is paid to the new breed of workers who use video screens and often entertain at the office. Small, two-level tables are made for supporting keyboards and video consoles. A low cabinet, looking like an old fashioned credenza, is a bar with a built-in refrigerator. Armoires, spindle-back chairs, and lamps with spun-metal shades complete the collection.

Work tops and legs are made of solid, hand-finished olive ash; side panels are polished black lacquer; stretchers on chairs, footrests on tables, and lamp stands are bent steel. Each piece is accented by a touch of red, such as the acrylic door handles and acid-etched glass.

If there is a kind of "now" feeling about this furniture, that may be because its shapes are familiar and its details remind us of humble things like metal screws and nylon nipples.

Photographs courtesy Johnny Grey

Photographs courtesy Sunar

Graves table

DESIGNER: Michael Graves

MANUFACTURER: Sunar, Waterloo, Ontario

In the 1980s the most public work that an architect can aspire to, second only to a major building, seems to be a showroom for a furniture manufacturer who also builds prototypes of his or her furniture designs. The Graves-Sunar collaboration began as the 1970s were about to become the 1980s, at the time when Sunar was reorganizing itself under new management. This resulted in a series of showrooms throughout metropolitan America, each one causing comment heard around the world. The word was out that a new sensibility was being created.

The ''sensibility'' was picturesque, emotional, and some even used such old-fashioned words as charming and beautiful. Coming at a time of general boredom and apathy in the furnishings industry, the Graves-Sunar team worked like a lightning rod. It electrified imaginations with its frankly decorative forms and colors. It made public a dialog of architectural inner circles that had, for twenty years, been debating the place of sensuality in design. And as messengers of the new era of feelings, the Graves-Sunar team began weighing its press clippings by the pound.

As a celebrity architect of the early 1980s, Graves built major buildings, won competitions for projects, and began designing furniture, then fabrics, for Sunar. The appeal of his work can be seen in his exquisite tables, which he says ''refer both to their anthropomorphic identification of our sitting position relative to them and the craft techniques of both former and present-day construction.''

The table, with its procession of

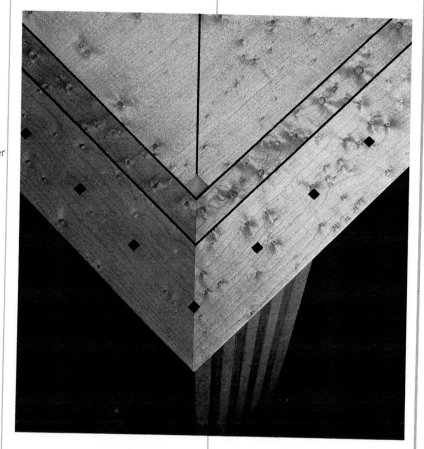

fluted, columnar legs that are reminiscent of colonnaded buildings, is appealing as a piece of furniture as well as a small piece of architecture. Its delicate top with its beaded-pattern bird's-eye maple veneers is decorated with inlays of ebony and mother-of-pearl. The same pattern is rendered in several painted versions, which the architect calls ''abstractions of the wood table.'' These are polyurethane-coated wood with lacquer squares and pinstripes.

Although the manufacturer hopes to produce many of these tables, the care that's needed in their crafting and the materials used make them somewhat rare pieces of furniture.

Conference table

DESIGNER/MAKER: Rosanne Somerson

GALLERY: Workbench, New York, New York

"I try to make furniture that entices the viewer's attention with a whisper. It may begin with the way a form slices into space or with the soft stance of a set of legs. Ideally, the presence of a piece of furniture becomes intimate and friendly company, so that when one walks into a room and senses the piece, even peripherally, little bits of pleasure subconsciously pool." So the young woman who was trained as an industrial designer describes her memorable work.

Her concern with the emotions is not at the expense of more practical considerations. In a conference table she made for the Park Avenue office of a New York executive, this dual sense of art and reality is admirably combined. The glass window on the top, she explains, provides an area for water pitcher and glasses while bringing the visual elements of the base directly to the top and allowing one to see the whole base from the top.

Made of curly maple and bubinga woods, accented by a thin, purled inlay that looks like gold embroidery, the table combines its maker's interest in "forms that have appeared in varied cultures and through many different periods of history," she says. "At present I'm exploring the positive tensions that can be constructed using simple geometric forms carefully aligned and misaligned."

Photographs by Susie Cushner

Photographs courtesy Gunlocke

Olympus desk

DESIGNER: Wendell Castle

MANUFACTURER: Wendell Castle/
The Gunlocke Company, Wayland,
New York

Since the 1960s, when he produced highly organic, laminated-wood forms that resembled nothing ever seen in furniture, Castle has been an important figure in the American crafts movement. His works, displayed in museums and now sold through galleries, are renowned for their creative explorations into the nature of materials, for their daring investigations of forms, and for pushing craftsmanship to its very finest, richest, and most emotionally satisfying limits. Now he has once again broken new ground with his series of limited edition desks, credenzas, and chairs, made under his supervision by a group of craftsmen and marketed by a well-known manufacturer of wood furniture. The Olympus desk—each edition is signed and numbered—is made in three woods: bubinga, East Indian rosewood, and teak.

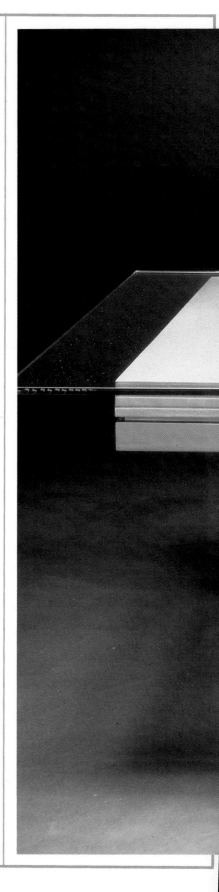

Extension table

DESIGNER/MAKER: Ed Zucca

GALLERY: Pritam & Eames, East Hampton, New York

The joy he takes in combining historical references from such diverse areas as Egyptian tombs and pre-Columbian architecture with the craftsmanship that rivals eighteenth-century skills of joinery is endearing Zucca's highly individual work to corporate executives. The extension table integrates such marvelously rich woods as Honduras mahogany, curly maple, prima vera, and ebony.

New Classics desk

DESIGNER: Dakota Jackson

MANUFACTURER: Dakota Jackson, Inc., Long Island City, New York

Early on in his career, Jackson became known as a "cult furniture maker," when combining his training in magic, dance, and art history, he built puzzlelike, mysteriously opening-closing desks for people like John Lennon. But all the while he has planned to become an industrialist who produces special furniture that combines high technology with craftsmanship. The newest group to come out of his factory includes tables, buffets, and desks that demonstrate a current fashion for classical references. Ebonized cherry legs with scored leather insets support slim drawers of leather and lacquer under the glass top; the crown caps are polished brass.

Photograph courtesy Pritam & Eames

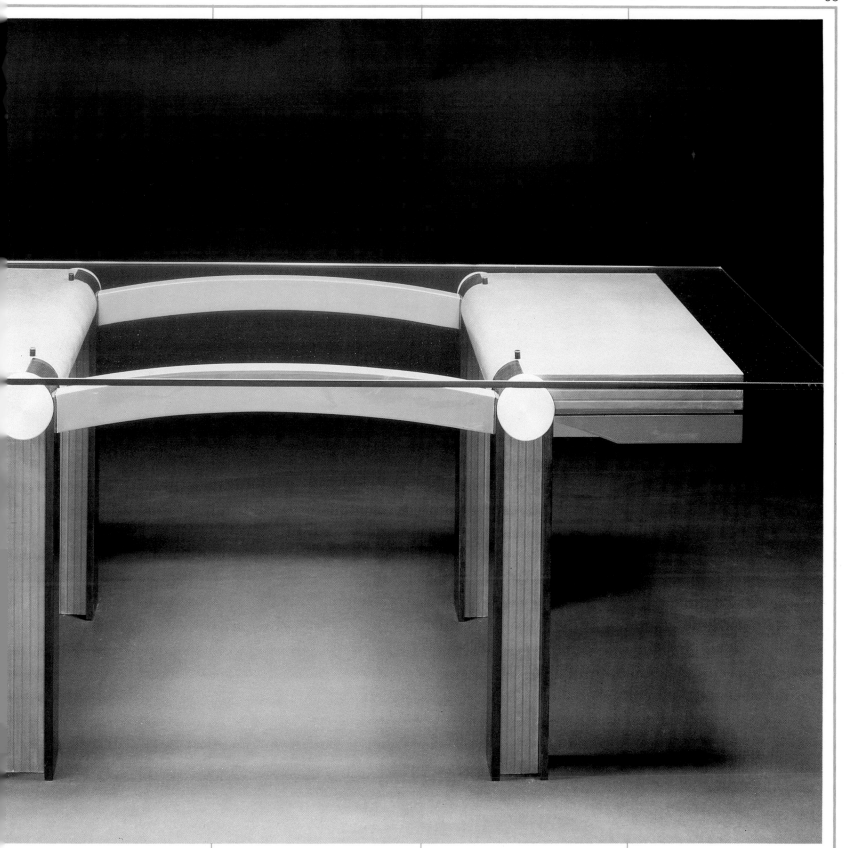

Photograph courtesy Dakota Jackson

Corner cabinet

DESIGNER/MAKER: George Gordon

GALLERY: Pritam & Eames, East Hampton, New York

Combining his training in architecture and furniture-making, Gordon designs simple forms that have a beautiful delicacy of detailing. The corner cabinet is made of curly maple, satin wood, and ebony.

Storage cubes

DESIGNER: Scott Burton

WORKSHOP: Scott Burton, New York, New York

Although the powerfully pure message of the Dutch avant-garde movement of the late 1910s and early 1920s continues to inspire the work of artists and architects, its missionary philosophy of utilitarianism is largely ignored. Writer and sculptor Burton, however, feels at ease combining art with function. His assembly of laminated wood cubes, which seem to float freely in midair, is also a storage cabinet.

Top photograph courtesy Pritam & Eames

Bottom photograph courtesy Protetch Gallery

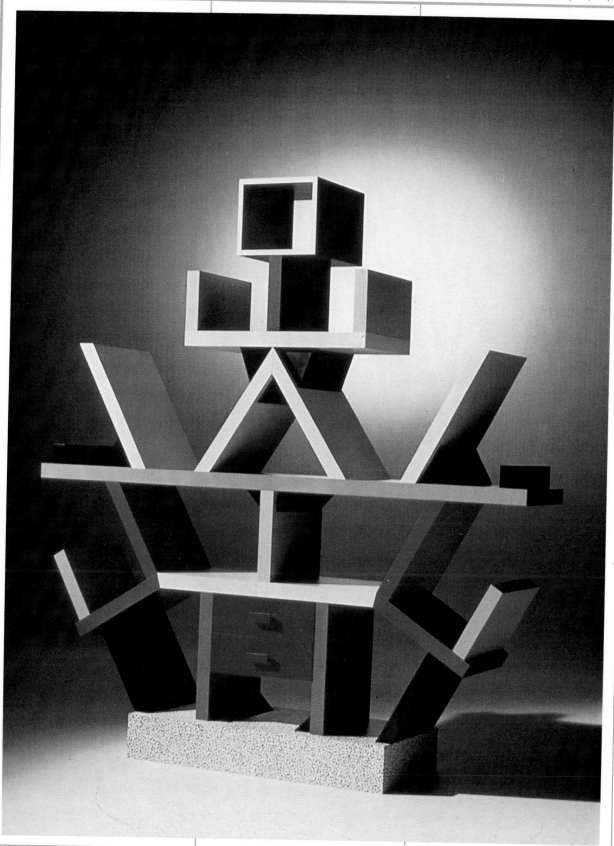

Carlton

DESIGNER: Ettore Sottsass

MANUFACTURER: Memphis, Milan;
Artemide, New York, New York

*As of 1980, all eyes seemed to be
fixed on Milan where an avant-garde
group of architects introduced their
assertive, colorful, and witty
furnishings designs as alternatives to
the industrial-production items that
they deemed dull and boring.
Although the new furniture uses
modern materials, like plastic
laminates, their eccentric shapes
require a great deal of handwork.
This and their highly individual forms
make Memphis' products uniquely
influential items that have become the
"new wave" couture line of the
furniture industry. The room divider
with bookshelves and drawers is
made of wood, covered with
patterned and colorful plastic
laminates. It can be disassembled,
like an erector set.*

Photograph courtesy Artemide

Armchair

DESIGNER: Peter Shire

MANUFACTURER: Memphis, Milan;
Artemide, New York, New York

*Wedge, cube, and cylinder forms are
assembled into an armchair that
makes definite demands on the other
furnishings in the room to keep quiet
and recede into the background.*

Photograph courtesy Artemide

Latis chair

DESIGNER: James Evanson

WORKSHOP: James Evanson, New York, New York

The designs of the Dutch avant-garde from 1917 are recalled in the hard lines and strong colors of these mysteriously tilting chairs. Aside from being highly decorative touches, the small, bright cylinders indicate important support points in the wooden chairs' architecture.

China Gothic chair

DESIGNER/MAKER: Jack Larimore

GALLERY: Workbench, New York, New York

Flexibility is built into chairs (and loveseats), which the designer describes as "sculpturally inspired by many traditions in seating but most strongly tied to Chinese aesthetic and the architecture and vestments of Gothic cathedrals." Casters at the bottom of the hardwood frame give it mobility. Under the seat, the latticed apron hides a drawer. The cushions are removable.

Top photograph by Jerry Sarapochiello

Bottom photograph by Rick Echelmeyer

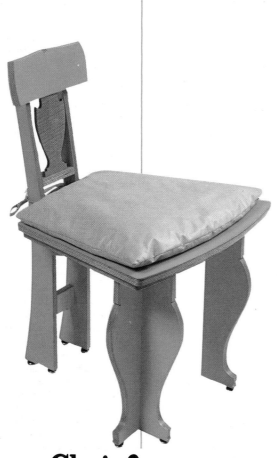

Chair 2

DESIGNER/MAKER: Trent Ravn
Whitington

GALLERY: Workbench, New York,
New York

*Because, as its maker says, the chair
is "loaded with esoteric symbolism,"
it may be enjoyed on several levels.
One person may like to catalog its
historical references; another may
simply delight in its eccentric shapes
and merry colors. Such individual
interpretation of his work is just fine
with the architect/sculptor who began
making furniture for himself, then for
others, as he matured from California
beach boy into a "responsible
dreamer." The materials are Baltic
birch plywood, curly maple veneer,
and housepaint.*

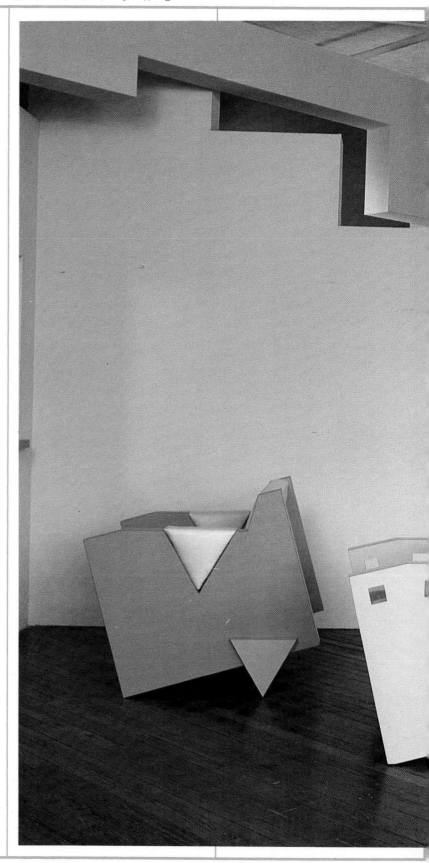

Photograph by Trent Whitington

Primazoid

DESIGNER: James Evanson

WORKSHOP: James Evanson, New York, New York

''It's not enough to design a chair that's merely comfortable. Your work should reflect the culture of your time—its excitement, passion, and mystery,'' says the young architect whose own work has been given such fashionably timely names as ''post-modern'' and ''new wave.'' But like other artists, he is impatient with labels and would rather concentrate on exploring his own media. For Evanson, that means a combination of painting, silk-screened graphics, interior architecture, and furniture design. The latter combines his architectural experiments with structure, balance, form, and detail with his painterly concerns for composition, graphics, and color. Each piece becomes a unique statement of contrasts.

Like his architecture, in which a supporting beam will alternate in an uninhibited pattern with a decorative beam, Evanson's furniture shows the same delightful combinations of rational and irrational elements. Perhaps more than anything else, these pieces express that rhythm and motion, that potentially confusing rotation, which may disturb some but enliven others who see this perpetual procession as the essence of modern life.

Photograph by Ronnie Kaufman

Useful Addresses

Furniture manufacturers

ARTEMIDE, INC.
150 East 58th Street
New York, NY 10155
212–980–0710

ATELIER INTERNATIONAL,
LTD.
595 Madison Avenue
New York, NY 10022
212–644–0400

B&B AMERICA/STENDIG
INTERNATIONAL, INC.
410 East 62nd Street
New York, NY 10021
212–838–6050

BEYLERIAN
305 East 63rd Street
New York, NY 10021
212–755–6300

BRICKEL ASSOCIATES, INC.
515 Madison Avenue
New York, NY 10022
212–688–2233

CASTELLI FURNITURE, INC.
950 Third Avenue
New York, NY
212–751–2050

CI DESIGNS
574 Boston Avenue
P.O. Box 191
Medford, MA 02155
617–391–7800

FURNITURE OF THE
TWENTIETH CENTURY
154 West 18th Street
New York, NY 10011
212–929–6023

GF FURNITURE SYSTEMS, INC.
Youngstown, Ohio
216–746–7271

THE GUNLOCKE COMPANY
One Gunlocke Drive
Wayland, NY 14572
716–728–5111

HERMAN MILLER, INC.
8500 Byron Road
Zeeland, MI 49464
616–772–3300

HOMEWORKS
107A Pimlico Road
London SW1, England
730–9116

INTERNATIONAL CONTRACT
FURNISHINGS, INC.
305 East 63rd Street
New York, NY 10021
212–750–0900

KINETICS FURNITURE
110 Carrier Drive
Rexdale, Ontario
Canada M9W 5R1
416–675–4300

KRUEGER, CONTRACT
DIVISION
P.O. Box 8100
Green Bay, WI 54308
414–468–8100

KNOLL INTERNATIONAL
655 Madison Avenue
New York, NY 10021
212–826–2400

LARSEN FURNITURE
41 East 11th Street
New York, NY 10003
212–674–3993

MEMPHIS S.R.L.
via Breda 1
20010 Pregnana (Milano)
Italy
02/93290663

METROPOLITAN FURNITURE
CORP.
950 Linden Avenue
South San Francisco, CA 94080
415–871–6222

NIENKAMPER
300 King Street East
Toronto, Ontario
Canada M5A 1KA
416–752–2575

PROBBER, HARVEY INC.
Fall River, MA 02722
617–674–3591

STENDIG INTERNATIONAL, INC.
410 East 62nd Street
New York, NY 10021
212-838-6050

STOW/DAVIS
25 Summer Avenue, N.W.
Grand Rapids, MI 49502
616-456-9681

SUNAR
One Sunshine Avenue
Waterloo, Ontario
Canada N2J4K5
519-886-2000

THONET
491 East Princess Street
P.O. Box 1587
York, PA 17405
717-845-6666

VECTA CONTRACT
1800 South Great Southwest Parkway
Grand Prairie, TX 75051
214-641-2860

Craftsmen and galleries

CASTLE, WENDELL
Alexander F. Milliken Gallery
98 Prince Street
New York, NY 10012
212-966-7800

EVANSON, JAMES
Architecture/Design
One Bond Street
New York, NY 10012
212-777-6943

GORDON, GEORGE
Pritam & Eames
29 Race Lane
East Hampton, NY 11937
516-324-7111

GREY, JOHNNY
Hampshire Farm
South Harting
Peterfield
Hampshire 9U31 5LP
England
073085-394

LARIMORE, JACK
325 Gaskill Street
Philadelphia, PA 19147
925-9294

SOMERSON, ROSANNE
173 Durnell Avenue
Roslindale, MA 02131
617-323-6320

WORKBENCH (THE GALLERY)
470 Park Avenue South
New York, NY 10016
212-481-5454

WHITINGTON, TRENT RAVN
64 West Cedar #4
Boston, MA 02114
617-742-8346

ZUCCA, ED
Pritam & Eames
29 Race Lane
East Hampton, NY 11937
516-324-7111

Bibliography

Albinson, Don, "Chair choice," *Industrial Design*, Nov./Dec. 1980, p. 41.

Brown, Patricia Leigh, "The chair behind the man," *Metropolis*, Jul./Aug. 1983, p. 12.

Busch, Akiko, "Annual Design Review," *Industrial Design*, Sept./Oct. 1983.

Caplan, Ralph, *By Design*, McGraw-Hill paperback, New York, 1984.

Chapman, Urbane, "Wendell Castle Tries Elegance," *Fine Woodworking* magazine, 1983 Taunton Press, Inc., Newton, CT.

Epstein, Jason, "The fine line from Pritam & Eames," *House & Garden*, Aug. 1983, p. 24.

Friedman, Martin, "Echoes of DeStijl," *De Stijl 1917–1931 Visions in Utopia*, Walker Art Center, Minneapolis, Abbeville Press, New York, 1982.

Giedion, Siegfried, *Mechanization Takes Command*, W.W. Norton & Company, New York, London, 1969.

Giovannini, Joseph, "Furniture for the post-modern interior," *The New York Times* Home section, Aug. 18, 1983.

Hiesinger, Kathryn B., *Design Since 1945*, catalog of Philadelphia Museum of Art Show, 1984.

Kaplan, Archie, "Designing with human factors is not a numbers game," *Industrial Design*, Jan./Feb. 1983.

Lucie-Smith, Edward, *Furniture, a concise history*, Oxford University Press, New York & Toronto, 1979.

Page, Marian, *Furniture Designed by Architects*, Whitney Library of Design, New York, 1980.

Papanek, Victor, *Design for the Real World*, Granada Publishing Ltd., London, Toronto, Sydney, New York, 1974.

Prete, Barbara, ed., *Chair*, produced by Peter Bradford, Thomas Y. Crowell, New York, 1978.

Smith, C. Ray and Marian Page, *The Wood Chair in America*, produced by Donovan & Green, published by Estelle D. Brickel & Stephen B. Brickel, New York, 1982.

Sottsass, Ettore, Jr., "When I was a child," *MANtransFORMS*, Smithsonian Institution, 1976.

Index

FOREST PARK LIBRARY